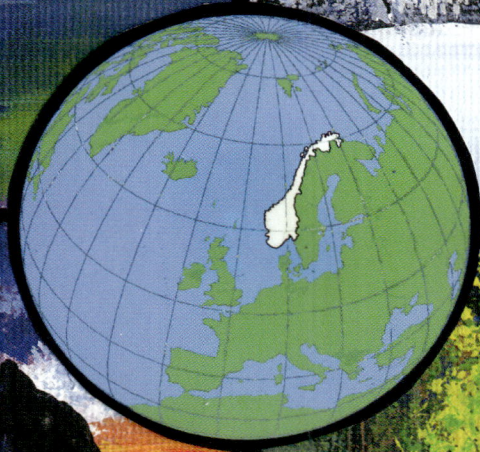

Published by:
Nordic Adventures
PO Box 11043 Olympia, WA 98508-8717
E-mail nordicadventures@comcast.net
www.NordicAdventures.com
1-800-618-0013 Fax 360 866-8717

First printing October 2005
10 9 8 7 6 5 4 3 2

Other books and videos by Astrid Karlsen Scott
Ekte Norsk Mat - Out of print
Ekte Norsk Jul Vol. I (Traditional Norwegian Christmas)
Ekte Norsk Jul Vol. II (Traditional Norwegian Christmas Foods)
Ekte Norsk Jul III Vol. III (Traditional Norwegian Christmas Songs, Stories and Poems)
Norway's Fest Days
Norway's Best (Cheese and other Delicacies)
Defiant Courage: Norway's longest WWII Escape, with Dr. Tore Haug
Little House on the Fjord
Silent Patriot: Norway's Most Highly Decorated WW II Soldier and Spy
Christmas in Norway - Video
Cooking Norway Style - Video

Printed in the United States of America by:
Publishers Book Services, Inc
PO Box 25334
Salt Lake City, Utah 84125
801-1972 5367

Yes, We Love This Land

Commemorating Norway's 100th Anniversary

Astrid Karlsen Scott

Edited by Debbie Majoros

Artwork by
Janice Montgomery
and Verna Paynter

Yes, We Love This Land

Norway is alive! From the towering mountains to the fjords, from the peaceful valleys to the ocean, from the bustling cities to the countryside; as with the land, so with the people – rugged yet mild, strong yet tender, proud yet modest.

Norway's spectacular fjords twist and turn from the sea for miles. Some days the violent sea thunders against the rockbound coast, while other days it laps lazily onto the rocky shore.

Norway is the daring fishermen, who carve out their existence by daily struggle with extreme cold, rough seas, even death.

Norway is the humble farmer with toil-worn hands, clearing the rocky land and daunting mountains, planting and harvesting for the long, unrelenting winter.

Norway is *seterjenta*, the dairymaid, at the mountain summit milking goats and cows, churning butter and making cheese for the dark wintry months ahead.

Norway is exhilarating winter: ice-skating, skiing, sledding; and the thrill of the snow sparkling like diamonds and crackling underfoot.

Norway is the cheerful warbling of the homecoming siskin, cuckoo, thrush and lark, and the eager watch for *gåselabber*, pussy willows, to open in the spring.

Norway is the delight of the *blåveis,* blue anemones, bravely poking their tiny heads through the snow and daring the wintry days to flee. And…

Norway is adventures and tales of folklore.

Frithjof Fure

A Land Far North

Norway, the northernmost country in Europe, extends along the Swedish boundary to the east and neighbors Finland and Russia to the northeast. The Barents Sea lies north, while the Norwegian Sea lies west and blends with the North Sea, which borders on the south. Norway also borders on the Atlantic Ocean to the southwest, and all along the 83.281-kilometer-long coast (including bays and fjords), embraces more than 50,000 islands.

Southern Norway is rather spherical and bunched up. But from Trondheim in central Norway all the way north to Kirkenes is a long and narrow outstretched land. By Tysfjord just south of Narvik at Hellemobotn the narrowest part in the country, there is only 6 km (approximately 3¾ miles) to the Swedish border.

Mountain ranges rise from the deep fjord waters and cover most of the land. A sparse population lives in the valleys and along the coastline. Many homes cling to steep mountainsides since only three percent of the land is arable.

One third of Norway lies above the Arctic Circle. For two and a half of the three months of snow-rich northern winters, the sun never rises. This makes the winters long, cold and dark – though clear nights reveal brilliant celestial planets, and the northern lights shimmer across fjords and mountain plateaus. The northern summers are filled with 24-hour-days of glorious sunlight; in southern Norway the daylight lingers for nineteen hours in the summer, but in the winters there are only six hours of daylight.

Norway is thought of as a cold land, but the Gulf Stream flows from the Caribbean Sea up along the Norwegian coast to the northern tip of Norway, making the land much warmer than Greenland and Alaska, which are on the same latitude.

Yet, Norway's inland is still cold. The cold forces the Norwegians inside in the winter. And this might be the reason why Norwegians love their homes and spend generously on layouts and furnishings.

Frithjof Fure

Spring

Spring's arrival varies throughout Norway, though May is thought of as the month of spring more than any other. When gurgling brooks break free of ice and the budding birch trees shroud the land in a verdant green, the Norwegians fling open windows and doors to bring the freshness of spring into their homes. Wild flowers, pussy willows and birch branches are gathered and brought inside.

The land awakens from winter's slumber and so do the people – it is the season of hope and high spirits. The city-folk take long hikes in the surrounding mountains and parks; the farmers till and prepare their fields and turn out their animals that have been confined all winter; and the aged venture on short walks nearer home. The children play outside and their laughter rings in the air.

Then the school children and the adults begin to sing the Norwegian patriotic songs:

Norway my Norway
Norway, my Norway, so soundly you sleep,
in winter's glittering halls
and no one can dream so pleasant and sweet
when the rivers sink into closing
and no one can smile so softly and glad
when the titmouse's warbling voice dies off,
And the woods repose in the valley.

Norway, my Norway! So give me your spring
With sun over the stirring waters.
But hear me, *ja,* hear me: at the day's end
when the evening shadow my brow.
Then teach me to wither, oh Norway, my mother!
and grant me a bed in your hallowed ground,
when the summer days leave our country.

English by Astrid Karlsen Scott

Norge, mitt Norge
Norge, mitt Norge, så sover du tyst
i vinterens skinnende sale,
og ingen kan drømme så lett og så lyst,
når elvene synker i dvale,
ingen kan smile så stille og glad
når meiserenes fløytende stemme dør av,
og skogen sover i dale.

Norge, mitt Norge! så giv meg din vår
med sol over vuggende vanne.
Men hør mig, ja, hør mig: når dagen forgår
og aftenen skygger min panne,
da lær meg å visne, å Norge, min mor!
og red mig en seng I din hellige jord,
når sommeren drager av lande.

Theodor Caspari

The Vikings

Long, long ago the Vikings governed Norway (800–1050 A.D.).

Though the Vikings were great artisans, skilled blacksmiths, traders, colonizers, poets, lawmakers and artists, they are often thought of as only fierce warriors. For more than 200 years the Vikings were feared as vicious and brutal pirates.

They expertly built vessels that could be both rowed and sailed, as well as withstand the mighty, turbulent waves of the open seas. The shallow-drafted vessels could easily travel through bays and inlets and be carried overland, enabling the Vikings to make surprise attacks.

They were great explorers and searched unidentified seas, and settled in unknown lands from Russia to east of Greenland; they settled the town of Dublin. The Vikings traversed the European coast, going as far as the Middle East and to America. Nearly 500 years before Columbus discovered America, Leif Erickson visited *Vinland*, which is believed to be present-day New Foundland. The Vikings did not settle there, most likely because of the native Indians.

When the fiercely-carved high-prow Viking ships with their square sails appeared on the horizon, panic broke out in the European coastal towns. Often the Vikings came to wreak havoc and plunder. But archaeological finds show that they traded peacefully as well, and that they were skilled craftsmen.

At home they were disciplined farmers and merchants. The Vikings excelled in agriculture, which they complemented with hunting and fishing.

Norway's Patron Saint

The last of the great Viking warriors, Olav Haraldsson, converted to Christianity in France during his travels. He returned home and conquered land held by the Norwegian lords - the Danes and the Swedes. At the age of nineteen he became king of Norway. In many ways he was a ruthless leader, but he upheld the laws of the land with fairness, and treated peasants and chieftains in like manner.

Olav Haraldsson determined to convert Norway to Christianity. Other leaders highly resented him for his Christian zeal, and he was forced to flee to Russia. When he felt the time was right, he left Russia and returned with a band of two hundred men. Along the way in Norway, many joined his ranks. His motley force of Christians and heathens are believed to have grown to four thousand men when they entered Stiklestad, a few miles from the Trondheimsfjord. In the midst of a gruesome hand-to-hand battle with swords, axes and javelins, King Olav fell at Stiklestad on July 29, 1030, some forty-five miles northeast of the city of Trondheim. It is said that he died in the warmth of the afternoon sun. His followers fled for their lives.

Alleged miracles happened almost immediately. Within a year he was recognized as a saint, and he became Norway's patron saint, St. Olav.

=====

In 1380, Denmark, Norway and Sweden were united under one king. By 1523 King Frederic I became King of Denmark-Norway. In January 1814, when the Treaty of Kiel was signed, King Frederic VI of Denmark-Norway was forced to cede Norway to Sweden. This ended the "400-year-night" union with Denmark.

Peter Nicolai Arbo

The Norwegian Constitution is Signed

At the beginning of 1814, Norway was an unsophisticated and isolated country on the periphery of Europe - poor and sparsely populated with about 900,000 inhabitants subject to Danish rule.

Up to then, anything of consequence concerning Norway had been decided in the Danish capitol of Copenhagen. With Denmark-Norway designated as an absolute monarchy, and the king himself approved all significant political decisions.

But the Norwegians now determined to choose their own rulers. In early April 1814, the well-liked Danish Commander-in-Chief, Christian Frederic, called together the Norwegian National assembly to meet at Eidsvoll, a manor house, belonging to Carston Anker and located some sixty kilometers north of Christiania (Oslo today).

On 11th of April, 112 men, average age forty-three years, from different walks of life, met with the purpose to negotiate Norway's Constitution. Nearly one-third of the assembly was farmers. In later years, a historian said, "Norway was a country without superiors, without leaders." It was hoped that the leaders would become known during the assembly. The delegates were all from the south; none were chosen from northern Norway due to the distance. Every delegate had his own agenda. Yet a singular spirit hovered over them, and within six challenging weeks, on May 17, 1814 they drafted and signed Norway's constitution, Europe's most liberal at the time.

The constitution the delegates adopted made a historic break with past traditions. The constitution, among other things, allowed the people to speak their minds frankly, to write and print what they wanted, so long as it was not offensive to modesty, religion or the king. And they were assured of the rule of law.

The delegates remained until May 20, 1814 when they promised each other to be, *"Enig og tro til Dovre faller,"* "United and true until Dovre (Mountains) fall."

The new national assembly was named the *Storting,* a name that had associations with the Old Norse word *ting,* which means legislative and judicial assembly of free men in Scandinavian Middle Ages. Its two chambers were called *Odelsting* (lower house of Norwegian legislature) and *Lagting,* (upper section of Storting) which also evoked memories of Norwegian history.

Sweden accepted the Norwegian constitution, and after a few weeks of minor skirmishes with the Swedes, Norway became united with Sweden under the Swedish king, Karl Johan XIV. Most Norwegians were not happy with this union.

Oscar Wergeland, 1887

Henrik Wergeland and Bjørnstjerne Bjørnson

For nearly a hundred years Norway was united with Sweden. But the spirit of independence was astir in the land and many patriots came to the forefront. Henrik Wergeland, a man much respected, an eloquent writer and poet worked diligently to make 17th of May a Norwegian national holiday, and to have it celebrated. He wrote a renowned song, "We Too are a Nation," also known as, "The Young Boys National Anthem." In 1833 he gave the first official Constitution Day speech in Oslo. When still a young man of thirty-seven he became ill with tuberculosis and pneumonia and died. On his last Constitution Day, people gathered outside his home to honor him.

We Too Are a Nation	*Vi ere en nasjon vi med*
We too are a nation,	Vi ere en nasjon vi med,
We youngsters so small,	vi små en alen lange,
We rejoice in our native land,	et fedreland vi frydes ved
And we, we are many.	Og vi, vi ere mange.
Our hearts know, our eyes can see	Vårt hjerte vet, vårt øye ser
How good and beautiful Norway is,	hvor godt og vakkert Norge er,
Our tongues know many words to	vår tunge kan en sang blant fler
Norway's glorious songs.	Av Norges æres sange.

Later Bjørnstjerne Bjørnson, one of the greatest poets Norway has ever known, and who wrote Norway's National Anthem, "Yes, We Love This Land of Ours," continued Henrik Wergeland's work. He also felt it was important to make Norway's Constitution Day a children's day. And he worked tirelessly to have 17th of May parades throughout the land for all children, and wrote songs for them to sing - songs loved to this day.

Yes, We Love This Land	*Ja, vi elsker dette landet*
Yes, we love this land of ours,	Ja, vi elsker dette landet,
As it rises forth	Som det stiger frem
Storm'lash'd o'er the sea it towers	furet værbitt over vannet
With its thousand homes.	med de tusen hjem,
Love it, love it ever thinking	elsker, elsker det og tenker
Of our parents dear	på vår far og mor
And the Saga-night that's lowering,	og den saga-natt som senker
Lowering dreams upon our soil.	senker drømme på vår jord,

Henrick Wergeland

Bjørnstjerne Bjørnson

Norway Chooses Her Own King

In 1905 the Norwegian Parliament dissolved the Swedish union deposed the union king without mentioning the monarchy, and that way they preserved a system of government. Norway's political leaders, backed by their voters, ably distinguished between the system and the person. But the *Storting* selected its new progenitor. They chose the Danish Prince Carl to be Norway's first king, following the dissolution with Sweden. This left no doubt that the Constitutional Government of 1905 was built on a democratic base.

Prince Carl would only assume the crown if he was accepted by a referendum, which he was. He arrived in Norway in November, 1905 with his English-Danish wife, Princess Maude, and their only child, three-year-old son, Alexander, who had been born in Appleton, England. Prince Carl took the name Haakon VII, and he gave his son an honored Norwegian name: Olav V.

At King Haakon's deputation on November 20th, 1905, when the *Storting* called him to be Norway's king, he told the Norwegian people the following: "I choose to consecrate my life to Norway. And it is my wife's and my fervent wish that the people who have chosen us, will in cooperation with us strive toward the good goals, and then with complete confidence I can take as my motto, 'All for Norway!'"

King Haakon was truly loved by the people of Norway until his death in 1957.

=====

Norwegians cherishing their freedom had managed to stay neutral during WWI, and they hoped for the same during WWII. This was not to be.

King Haakon VII and Crown Prince Olav's arrival in Norway, November 1905

Norway is Invaded

On April 9, 1940 Germany, sustained by her mighty Luftwaffe air force, invaded Norway in the early hours before dawn. Some one thousand German fighter planes, reconnaissance and transport planes engaged in the attack. The Germans secretly moved their armada of warships northward toward Narvik above the Arctic Circle, capturing the major coastal towns and communications centers along the way. They sailed up the sixty- three-mile long Oslofjord toward Oslo. Hitler's plot was to take the king and the government captive.

In the Oslofjord, when the warships reached the Drøbaksundet Sound, the strait that must be passed through to get to Oslo by boat, the artillery at Oscarsborg Fortress fired on the German troop ship Blüchner and scored hits. The ship went down with more than 1000 men. This gave the king and the government leaders precious moments to escape inland on their first step on the way to England.

Untrained and unprepared to fight the world's greatest army at the time, the Norwegians in the south soon had to surrender. In the north, however, due to the courage of General Gustaf Fleicher - who took it upon himself to mobilize 10,000 men - they battled the Germans for two months in the Arctic mountains of Troms. With the Allies they fought a bitter and brave fight, and drove the Germans close to the Swedish border and internment.

But on June 8, 1940 when France and Holland fell, the Allies were called home and the Norwegians were ordered to demobilize. Many of the men felt betrayed - that the Allies' courage and sacrifice, and their own, had no value. Gloom spread, and many men broke down and cried. Norway was lost! For five terrifying years Norway was under the Nazi regime, which had swelled to over 350,000 soldiers at the end of the war, guarding a nation with just under four million people. That is when the sacredness of freedom truly dawned on Norway.

Germans invade Norway, April 9, 1940

Today Our Flagpole Stands Naked

Nordahl Grieg, poet, dramatist and journalist, volunteered for active duty when war came to Norway. Grieg served in Norway's government-in-exile and made and sent patriotic radio programs from England to Norway. He wrote never-to-be-forgotten poetry about freedom that was circulated among the Norwegian people during the war. In 1943, as an observer, he joined a bombing mission over Germany. The plane was shot down December 2nd of that year. Among Nordahl Grieg's most loved patriotic poems is:

Today Our Flagpole Stands Naked.

Today our flagpole stands naked
Among Eidsvoll's budding trees.
But just in this hour
we know what freedom is.
There rises a song over the land,
victorious in its speech,
though whispered with closed lips
beneath the strangers' yoke.

A knowing is born within us;
Freedom and life are one,
So simple, so essential
As the people's right to breathe.
We felt when the thralldom threatened
That our lungs gasped in need
As in a sunken U-boat…
We will not die such a death.

Here we shall remember the dead
Who gave their lives for peace.
The soldier in blood on the snow,
The seaman who sank in the sea.
We are so few here in our land:
Each fallen is brother or friend
We have the dead with us
the day we come again.

I Dag Står Flagstangen Naken

I dag står flagstangen naken
blant Eidsvolls grønnende trær.
Men nettop I denne timen
vet vi hva frihet er.
Der stiger en sang over landet,
seirende I sitt språk,
skjønt hvisket med lukkede leber
Under de fremmedes åk.

Det fødtes I oss en visshet;
Frihet og liv er ett,
så enkelt så uunnværlig
Som menneskets ånderett.
Vi følte da trelldommen truet
At lungene gispet I nød
som I en sunken u-båt…
Vi vil ikke dø slik en død.

Her skal vi minnes de døde
som gav sitt liv for fred.
Soldaten i blod på sneen,
Sjømannen som gikk ned.
Vi er så få her I landet:
Hver fallen er bror og venn.
Vi har de døde med oss

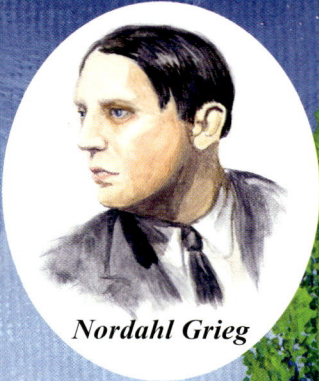

Nordahl Grieg

Eidsvoll Building where Constitution was signed 1814

Our Fighting Men and Women During WW II

Anger arose in the hearts of the Norwegian people, especially the idealistic youth. They fought back in various ways. Many were captured, tortured and executed, and others escaped to England, where they trained as commandoes and returned to Norway on secret missions. For example:

Knut Haukelid and his small but courageous group of Norwegian commandoes successfully sabotaged the "heavy water" plant (the water contained heavy hydrogen to be used in a nuclear reactor). The plant was located at Rjukan, in Telemark, and was vital to Hitler's race with the United States to develop the atom bomb. Knut Haukelid and his men sabotaged the ferry with the "heavy water" while in transport to Germany on Tinnsjø Lake, Telemark. It was a heart-rending descision because many Norwegians were aboard. In his book, "A Man called Intrepid" Chief of the British Security Coordination (BSC) William Stevenson said, "If it had not been for Haukelid's resolve, the Germans would have had the opportunity to devastate the civilized world. We would be either dead or living under Hitler's zealots." Knut was highly decorated by Norway, Britain, France, Sweden and the United States.

Hugo Munthe-Kaas, at 18 became the youngest volunteer-recruit in the brutal campaign in northern Norway in 1940. Later, trained as a commando in England, he was sent back to Norway on seven missions. On his first mission he set up a radio network to track Germany's largest warship, the *Tirpitz,* which was sunk outside of Tromsø in 1944. That same year he parachuted into Vassfaret, Norway to help set up guerilla bases to train underground Milorg men (a military resistance force) for the last battle against Hitler's army in Norway. At the war's end, when Hugo was twenty-three years old, Britain, France and Norway had decorated him highly.

Jan Baalsrud, was one of four Norwegians selected for an extremely dangerous and top-secret commando operation in northern Norway. The Norwegian Commandoes trained in the Scottish Highlands and arrived in northern Norway on a 72-foot fishing vessel with eight tons of explosives in the hull. A Norwegian shopkeeper betrayed the saboteurs, and a German Schnell-boat attacked the cutter, turning the quiet fjord into a battle zone. Ultimately, only Jan survived the attack. Wounded, he began his escape through the Arctic where he suffered with snow-blindness, got caught in an avalanche, and sustained a concussion, and gangrene attacked his feet. More than sixty people, selflessly defying Nazi dictates, risked their lives to help the fugitive reach freedom in Sweden after two months in hiding. He then weighed only seventy-eight pounds.

Erik Reichelt, since the beginning of the war, had been involved in intelligence work and in transport of fugitives in Tønsberg and in the Oslo area. He left Norway in 1942, but returned several times on secret missions. He was part of the Baalsrud operation and was horribly tortured before he died in the hospital, without revealing any secrets.

Anne-Margrethe Bang became known as the, "WAC from Hegra." For 26 days she used her first-aid knowledge - learned from her surgeon-father when she was twelve - on the 250 men she was interned with at Fort Hegra. Like the men, she slept on a wet straw sack with a thin blanket, getting about four hours of sleep a night. It was one of the coldest winters on record, and Anne Margrethe had to have several toes amputated because of frostbite. The Hegra men and Anne-Margrethe were all taken prisoners. After Anne-Margrethe was released, she worked in the underground.

Anne-Margrethe Bang

Erik Reichelt

Knut Haukelid

Jan Baalsrud

Hugo Munthe-Kaas

Peace Returns To Norway

Celebration broke out instantly when Norway was liberated on May 8th, 1945 and prisoners were set free. Euphoric people poured from their homes and buildings to gather in their towns' squares; streets filled, making it nearly impossible to move about. Strangers became friends, sharing struggles they had endured throughout the war. It would take time to learn to live without fear again.

But on this day, all of Norway was singing songs forbidden for five terrifying years. The beautiful Norwegian flag fluttered freely from streetcars, buses, trains, cars, flagpoles, balconies and baby carriages. The people carried hand flags, and red, white and blue ribbons pinned on their lapels turned the land into a field of color.

Nine days later, on the 17th of May, Norway's Constitution Day, the celebration intensified. The observance began in the predawn hours as the graduating students rumbled up and down the streets in old trucks, or beat-up cars decorated with birch branches and flags. The people dressed in whatever finery they had. By early morning, the public either took part in, or viewed, the parades with all the school children and their brass bands.

Speeches were given; the people danced in the streets, hugged and laughed, and ate the best food obtainable from post-war supplies. The celebration never ceased for a month. Norway was free, and the fervor of the grateful people was unstoppable.

Norwegians had learned that the freedom newly recovered to their land was sacred, and that this precious God-given gift was built on sacrifice.

How 17ᵗʰ of May is Celebrated Today

The 17ᵗʰ of May is still synonymous with celebration, and is observed all over the world wherever Norwegians are found. In larger Norwegian cities, early-morning revelry begins as students rush through the streets in decorated cars and trucks. In Oslo school children from 110 schools march, sing and wave their flags to shouts of *"Hurra, hurra, hurra!"* and file past the Royal Palace to salute the Royal Family

May 17ᵗʰ has remained the great spring festival, in a country where the winters are long, dark and cold. The children's parade is the central point of the celebration from the most far-flung coastal settlements to Oslo, the capitol city where literally thousands of school children march behind their school bands and banners. People dress in national costumes. Homes and office buildings are decorated in the color of the flag and birch branches, which are a symbol of spring. Norway is aglow, ready to welcome its Constitution day.

The foods are festive; cured meats, scrambled eggs with chives, a dab of sour cream, open-face sandwiches, hot dogs with *lumpe* (small potato cake), and cakes galore with plenty of ice cream. For recipes see www.NordicAdventures.com.

Kransekake

Norway Today

The year 2005 represents 100 years since Norway's dissolution with Sweden, and 60 years following WWII. The Norwegian people have re-established their freedom and have risen economically from the ashes to become one of the world's wealthiest nations, due in part to rich oil and gas resources in the North Sea.

Oil industry: In little more than 30 years Norway has developed a petroleum industry with world-class products and solutions. Out of a population of 4.5 million people, some 75,000 people work in the oil industry. Norway holds the position of being the 2nd largest exporter of oil after Saudi Arabia. The country has established a unique Petroleum Fund, which currently has passed $260 billion. World leaders in resource rich oil companies are looking to Norway for inspiration and guidance.

Service: The government sends individuals to third world nations to train and educate, and give agricultural support to developing countries. The Norwegians send their young soldiers on peace-keeping missions, and have since 1947 contributed military personnel to more than 30 international operations and special forces to Enduring Freedom.

Architecture: In 1988 UNESCO organized an architectural competition to choose a design worthy of the site and the heritage of the old Alexandria Library, Egypt. The Norwegian architectural firm, Snøhetta was chosen from among more than 1400 entries to design the new library. Biblotheea Alexandria officially opened October 16, 2002. Snøhetta was also chosen from a pool of 34 aspirants to design the memorial cultural center to be built on the sight of the collapsed World Trade Center.

Tunnel Builders: Norway is the world leader in building tunnels. The country's road system has over 915 tunnels. It has the deepest, and the longest road tunnel, 24.5 kilometers in Lærdal.

Chefs: Norwegian chefs have one silver and three gold medals in the culinary championships at the Bocuse d'or France. The world's largest culinary championship, established in 1987 by Paul Bocuse, the world's most renowned chef.

Sports: Most will remember the Winter Olympic Games in Lillehammer, Norway in 1994. According to The Golden Book of Olympic Games, Norway has the highest All-Winter Games medals (263).

Music: Violinist, Arve Tellefsen, has toured the world extensively. His ability to captivate and communicate ranks him among the greatest violinists in the world today. Sissel, in Norway her recordings are national events. Her pure beautiful voice is acclaimed around the world. She has performed with Placido Domingo in a Christmas concert in Vienna, with the Mormon Tabernacle on Temple Square in Salt Lake City, Utah, and she sang the hymn in the opening and closing Winter Olympics in 1994. She travels and performs across the world.

With these few examples we see that the Norwegians have learned from their history, to use each moment *to* serve, to improve their lives, and to share skills and talents. To quote King Harald V, "Norway cannot afford to forget its past. If so, we stand in danger of losing our best traditions. There might be times when we have to stand up to protect our worth. Moreover, many of our approaches to the happenings and events of our times, are more simple to understand if one knows one's own history."

The Norwegians have learned that freedom has a price, and it is built on strong traditions, historical values, and benevolence to others, and the great worth of every human being.

"Go to the land with the heaven aglow
Go to the home of troll and the snow
Lead your dream by the hand
to wonderland."

From the song, "Fire in the Heart."

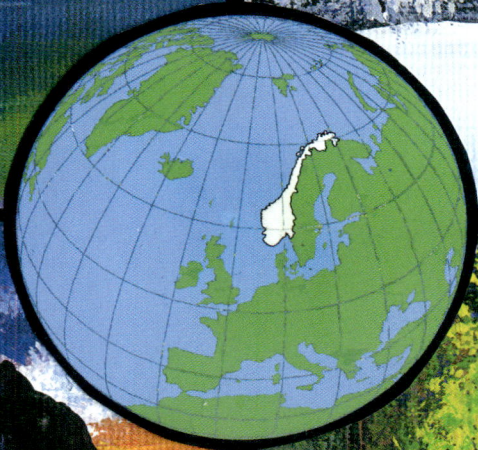